Supercharge Your Leadership:

A Path to Personal Power and Professional Success

By

Victoria Renard

Disclaimer

Table of Contents

This table of topics presents a methodical blueprint for readers to travel their journey toward personal power and professional success via effective leadership.

Introduction

Leadership is more than a job title; it's a superpower waiting to be released. In **'Supercharge Your Leadership: A Path to Personal Power and Professional Success,'** we're going to disclose the secret recipe for converting ordinary professionals into extraordinary leaders. Buckle up, for your trip to power and success begins now!

The Power of Leadership.

Leadership is a dynamic force that affects individuals, teams, organizations, and even countries. It contains the potential to inspire, influence, and drive change.

At its basis, leadership is about directing a group of people toward a shared aim, and its effect is substantial.

First and foremost, leadership empowers individuals to fulfill their highest potential. A successful leader can recognize and cultivate the qualities and abilities of the people they lead, helping them develop and achieve set goals. This empowerment not only benefits the people but also increases the overall capacity and performance of the team or organization.

Leadership also sets the tone for the culture and values of a group or enterprise. A strong leader can develop a culture of trust, openness, and accountability, encouraging a healthy working environment. Conversely, poor leadership can lead to a poisonous climate that hampers productivity and innovation.

In addition, leadership influences decision-making. Leaders are typically accountable for making key choices that determine the direction and performance of their businesses. Their capacity to make informed, smart judgments can lead to prosperity, while incorrect decisions might result in setbacks.

Moreover, leadership plays a significant function in motivating and inspiring others.

A charismatic leader may organize their team in the face of adversity, establishing a feeling of purpose and drive.

This inspiration is a driving force that may lead to amazing achievements.

Ultimately, the strength of leadership comes from its potential to produce good change. Effective leaders can imagine a better future, define a path toward that goal, and push their people to turn it into reality. They may stimulate innovation, nurture development, and leave a lasting legacy.

In essence, leadership is a changing force that impacts people, organizations, ·and the world at large. Its strength resides in its capacity to empower, influence, and inspire, making it a critical element in the pursuit of personal and communal accomplishment.

Part 1

Self-discovery

Self-discovery is a very personal and transforming journey that entails obtaining a great insight into oneself. It's an exploration of one's values, beliefs, strengths, flaws, interests, and purpose in life. This process of self-discovery can be a lifelong endeavor, and it's crucial for personal growth and joy.

One of the primary components of self-discovery is understanding one's values and beliefs.
What principles influence your life? What do you stand for? These questions help shape your identity and drive your decision-making. When you match your activities with your fundamental values, you frequently experience a stronger sense of authenticity and contentment. Recognizing your strengths and inadequacies is another crucial component of self-discovery. Knowing what you

excel at may help you make the most of your talents while embracing your deficiencies helps you to

focus on personal growth and development. It's a route to becoming the best version of yourself.

Passions and hobbies are also a significant component of self-discovery. Exploring what delights and inspires you could lead to a more fulfilled life. Your interests can serve as a compass, leading you toward activities and pursuits that provide you pleasure and fulfillment.

Self-discovery isn't only about self-analysis; it's also about setting objectives and finding your purpose. What do you want to accomplish in life, and how do you want to have a good influence on the world? Finding your life's purpose may provide you with a feeling of direction and motivation.

Self-discovery typically requires introspection, self-reflection, and sometimes even seeking the guidance of mentors, therapists, or coaches. It takes a desire to study your inner thoughts and emotions, and it may mean going out of your comfort zone to undertake new experiences.

In the end, self-discovery is a powerful path that leads to a stronger sense of self-awareness and a more meaningful, purpose-driven life. It allows you to better understand who you are, what you desire, and how you may make a constructive contribution to the world. It's a tour of personal growth and a path to live a life that is both authentic and meaningful.

Chapter 1

Effective Steps to Knowing Yourself.

In this chapter of our journey towards self-discovery, we will go into the heart of the matter: knowing yourself. It is here that we set the basis for the transforming trip ahead. Self-awareness is the key that opens the doors to personal progress, happiness, and success.

Below are 13 effective steps that will assist in fully knowing yourself:

1. Self-Reflection: Dedicate time for contemplation. Regularly ponder your ideas, emotions, and

experiences. Journaling may be a good instrument for self-reflection.

2. Seek feedback: Ask for opinions from friends, family, and coworkers. They may give substantial insights into your strengths and shortcomings.

3. Assess Your Values: Identify your basic values and beliefs. Consider what principles drive your life and what matters most to you.

4. Identify Strengths and Weaknesses: Reflect on your talents and abilities. Recognize your talents to exploit them and identify weaknesses to work on personal progress. By recognizing your strengths, you'll utilize your innate ability to attain your goals. Simultaneously, understanding your vulnerabilities will allow you to go on a journey of personal improvement and growth.

5. Explore Interests: Discover your hobbies and interests. Engage in things that excite and drive you. Your passions often indicate your actual personality.

6. Set objectives: Define short-term and long-term objectives. Goals create a feeling of purpose and direction in life.

7. Embrace obstacles: Face your worries and obstacles. Overcoming barriers may lead to self-discovery and personal improvement.

8. Self-Assessment Tools: Use self-assessment tools like personality tests or job assessments to get insights into your preferences and inclinations.

9. Meditation and Mindfulness: Practice meditation and mindfulness to connect with your inner self, ease stress, and improve clarity.

10. Seek Guidance: Consider seeking the guidance of a therapist, counselor, or coach. They may give expert advice and aid in your journey for self-discovery.

11. Learn from Life experiences: Pay attention to your life events, both joyful and unpleasant. They frequently offer significant lessons about your beliefs and objectives.

12. Network and Build Relationships: Interacting with diverse individuals may help you comprehend alternative viewpoints and learn more about yourself via social interactions.

13. Continual Learning: Engage in lifelong learning. New information and experiences may increase your self-awareness.

Remember, self-discovery is a continuing process. It needs patience, self-compassion, and a desire for personal improvement. By adopting these practical steps, you may obtain a greater understanding of yourself and live a more real and meaningful life.

Chapter 2

Defining Your Leadership Style

This chapter is your guide to understanding the unique leadership strategy that best suits you. Explore leadership styles, from visionary to collaborative, and learn how to adapt them to diverse situations. This will help you obtain insights on how to effectively lead and influence people, establishing the groundwork for your personal leadership path.

Effective leadership may take different forms, depending on the context and the expectations of the team or organization.

Here are some effective leadership styles:

1. **Transformational Leadership**: Leaders inspire and push their team by establishing a compelling vision and cultivating a sense of

purpose. They promote innovation and personal development.

2. **Servant Leadership**: Leaders value the well-being and progress of their team members. They concentrate on serving the needs of others and frequently lead by example.

3. **Democratic Leadership**: This approach combines cooperation and shared decision-making. Leaders solicit feedback from the team before making decisions, generating inclusion and agreement.

4. **Autocratic Leadership**: In circumstances necessitating swift choices and clear direction, leaders utilize a more authoritarian approach. They make decisions unilaterally and expect complete respect for their commands.

5. **Laissez-Faire Leadership**: Leaders in this style provide great autonomy to team members. It works well when the team is highly talented and self-motivated.

6. **Transactional Leadership**: This technique focuses on organized transactions between leaders and followers. It often incorporates incentives and punishments depending on performance.

7. **Charismatic Leadership**: Charismatic leaders possess a strong presence and can inspire and influence others via their personal appeal and captivating communication.

8. **Situational Leadership**: Leaders adjust their approach to the unique demands of each scenario or person. They determine what leadership style is most appropriate depending on the circumstances.

9. **Coaching Leadership**: Leaders take on a mentoring role, enabling team members to realize their heightened potential via continuous feedback and support.

10. **Authentic Leadership**: Authentic leaders lead with honesty, transparency, and a strong sense of self. They are sincere and devoted to their values.

Productive leaders generally apply a combination of different techniques depending on the environment and the people they are leading. The key to effective leadership is the ability to flexibly use the correct style at the right moment to produce the highest outcomes for the team and organization.

Chapter 3

Unleashing Your Inner Leader.

Unleashing your inner leader includes more than only the frequently mentioned suggestions.

Here are some lesser-discussed concepts to help you tap into your leadership potential:

1. **Embrace Sensitivity**: Leaders don't need to generate all the answers. It's good to confess when you don't know something and seek ideas from others. Vulnerability may promote trust and cooperation.
2. **Practice Active Listening**: Truly listening to others, without interrupting or constructing your answer, is a vital but generally disregarded leadership talent. It communicates respect and understanding.

3. **Learn from Failure**: Embrace failures and setbacks as beneficial learning experiences.

A resilient leader can transform tragedies into opportunities for development and progress.

4. **Cultivate Emotional Agility**: Emotional intelligence is crucial, but so is emotional agility. It entails not only identifying your emotions but also being adaptive and receptive to altering emotional states.

5. **Mentorship**: Seek mentorship or become a mentor. Learning from seasoned leaders or aiding others on their leadership path may provide unique insights and development potential.

6. **Cross-Cultural Competence**: In today's variegated world, leading across numerous cultures and backgrounds is vital. Understanding and respecting cultural nuances may be a fantastic leadership benefit.

7. **Continual Learning**: Continuously engage in your personal and professional growth. A devotion to continual learning keeps your leadership qualities fresh and relevant.

8. **Networking Beyond Your Industry**: Building links with individuals from various professions

helps extend your viewpoint and give new ideas to your leadership style.

9. **Quiet Leadership**: Recognize that leadership is not always about taking control. Sometimes, being a quiet leader by supporting others and allowing them to shine is as successful.

10. ** Appreciation**: Expressing thanks and appreciation for your team's efforts is frequently disregarded but may enhance morale and establish lasting ties.

Unleashing your inner leader is a dynamic process that includes ongoing self-discovery and improvement. These less-discussed strategies may complement the more prevalent ideas and help you become a powerful and genuine leader.

Part II

Building Personal Power.

Establishing personal power comprises self-confidence, communication skills, and emotional intelligence.

It's about gaining the inner strength to conquer challenges, make assertive choices, and inspire others, eventually leading to massive personal and professional breakthroughs.

Chapter 4

Mastering Self-Confidence

Mastering self-confidence is a process. It needs time and practice to manifest.

Here are some strategies to boost your self-confidence:

1. Positive Self-Talk: Replace self-doubt with positive affirmations and ideas.

2. Set Achievable Goals: Small successes generate confidence over time.

3. Embrace Failure: Learn from failures; they're part of progress.

4. Self-Care: A healthy body and mind encourage confidence. So embrace self-care and well-being to boost overall self-esteem.

5. Preparation: Thoroughly prepare for tasks or challenges.

6. Body Language: Maintain excellent posture and eye contact.

7. Face Your Fears: Tackle what you're terrified of gradually.

8. Visualize Success: Mental rehearsal may increase confidence.

9. Seek Feedback: Use constructive criticism as a development tool.

10. Appreciate wins: Acknowledge and appreciate your successes.

11. Surround Yourself with Positivity: Be around supporting and optimistic individuals as the lifters.

The lifters are filled with positivity and are always questing for overall growth. They are actively involved, highly focused, and always seek the best solutions while standing up for what they believe. They genuinely enjoy responsibility because they know its importance. Relate more with them and see positivity improve your mindset.

Avoid the set of persons outlined below for your overall growth:

i) The Loafers: They are unpunctual, lack note-taking equipment, a heightened degree of indifference with many other bad attitudes that inhibit achievement. They will only prevent you from noticing possibilities coming your way, stifle your potential, and add to your misfortune.

ii) The Leech: Don't mutually associate with those unwilling to seek solutions and innovation but are more than willing to reap from the gain of your labor. They are jocund yet make no real sacrifice to achieve fruition. They are obedient workers who always aim to dwell in the good grace of influential people to maintain their jobs.

They rarely think of new hunches and snatch others' ideas, sometimes claiming them to be theirs. They can steal your opportunity to raise themselves. They can't be a catalyst of wins.

12. Seek Professional Help: Consider therapy or counseling if low self-confidence is a recurring problem.

13. Practice Gratitude: Recognize and appreciate your abilities and successes.
14. Visualize Success: Imagine yourself succeeding in your activities. It gives you the motivation to keep trying until you reach your target.
Remember, self-confidence is a skill promoted over time.

Chapter 5

Effective Communication

Effective communication is a cornerstone of triumph in both personal and professional life.

Here are some excellent recommendations to increase your communication skills:

1. **Active Listening**: Pay full attention to the speaker and reply intelligently.

2. **Clarity and Conciseness**: Express your views simply and succinctly, avoiding extraneous jargon.

3. **Empathy**: Understand and appreciate the emotions and opinions of others.

4. **Non-Verbal Communication**: Be careful of your body language, gestures, and facial expressions.

5. **Adaptability**: Tailor your communication approach to your audience's requirements and preferences.

6. **Feedback**: Seek and offer constructive feedback for continued progress.

7. **Use of Questions**: Ask open-ended questions to foster conversation and improve knowledge.

8. **Confidence**: Speak with confidence, but avoid arrogance or aggression.

9. **Avoid Assumptions**: Clarify when in doubt and avoid making assumptions about what others want.

10. **Stay Calm Under Pressure**: Maintain calm amid stressful or emotional conversations.

11. **Respect quiet**: Don't hurry to fill gaps in talk; silence may be profound.

12. **Cultural Sensitivity**: Be sensitive to cultural variations in communication strategies and norms.

13. **Use of Technology**: Master digital communication tools and etiquette.

14. **Positive Body Language**: Maintain eye contact, smile, and assume open postures.

15. **Authenticity**: Be yourself and communicate from the heart.

Effective communication is a talent developed over time. By concentrating on these principles, you may establish vast, more meaningful connections and achieve exceptional wins in your interactions with others.

Chapter 6

Emotional Intelligence

Building emotional intelligence (EI) is a primary quality for personal and professional victory.

Here are 50 practical and powerful methods to boost EI:

1. **Self-Awareness**: Regularly reflect on your emotions, triggers, and reactions to gain knowledge of your emotional responses.

2. **Mindfulness**: Practice being present in the moment, which helps you understand and regulate your emotions.

3. **Empathy**: Put yourself in others' position to grasp their emotions and opinions.

4. **Active Listening**: Pay entire attention while individuals are speaking to grasp their feelings.

5. **Manage Stress**: Learn stress management methods to stop emotions from dominating you.

6. **Self-Regulation**: Control impulsive emotional responses and adopt more productive ones.

7. **Social abilities**: Work on your communication and conflict resolution talents to establish better connections.

8. **Recognize Emotions in Others**: Learn to detect others' emotions properly.

9. **Flexibility**: Be adaptable and open to alternative viewpoints and ways of accomplishing things.

10. **Develop Perseverance**: Bounce back from setbacks and disappointments, viewing them as chances for development.

11. **Seek input**: Request input from others to discover how your actions and emotions affect others.

12. **Practice Empathetic Listening**: Listen not just to words but also to sentiments in others' voices and body language.

13. **Self-Reflection**: Regularly analyze your emotional reactions and their impact on your decisions.

14. **Boundary Setting**: Set appropriate emotional boundaries to protect your well-being.

15. **Conflict Resolution Skills**: Develop effective techniques to manage and resolve disagreements.

16. **Cultural Sensitivity**: Understand and respect cultural differences in emotional expression.

17. **Gratitude**: Practice gratitude to maintain a positive emotional state.

18. **Manage Impatience**: Cultivate patience to deal with delays and unforeseen events calmly.

19. **Leadership**: Apply EI in leadership roles to inspire and motivate teams.

20. **Appreciate Diverse Perspectives**: Value the diverse emotional experiences of others.

21. **Emotion Journal**: Maintain a journal to monitor your emotional experiences and triggers.

22. **Practice Mindful Communication**: Engage in deliberate, compassionate conversations.

23. **Non-Verbal Cues**: Pay attention to non-verbal signs for deeper emotional insights.

24. **Emotion Regulation Techniques**: Learn relaxation, meditation, or deep-breathing exercises.

25. **Conflict Resolution**: Learn constructive strategies to address issues and establish stronger relationships.

26. **Respect Personal Boundaries**: Understand and respect the emotional boundaries of others.

27. **Authenticity**: Be sincere and honest about your inner emotions.

28. **Practice Empathetic Responses**: Respond to others' feelings with empathy and support.

29. **Forgiveness**: Learn to forgive and let go of previous emotional traumas.

30. **Recognize Emotional Manipulation**: Be mindful of emotional manipulation strategies in relationships.

31. **Adapt to Change**: Embrace change as a chance for growth and learning.

32. **Emotional Courage**: Be willing to tackle grim emotions and situations.

33. **Self-Compassion**: Treat yourself with the same kindness you'd extend to a friend.

34. **Manage Impulsivity**: Avoid hasty decisions by taking time to assess emotions and facts.

35. **Conflict Mediation**: Develop abilities to arbitrate conflicts in personal and professional situations.

36. **Positive Self-Image**: Cultivate healthy self-esteem to promote overall emotional well-being.

37. **Balance Assertiveness with Empathy**: Find the perfect balance between sticking up for yourself and considering others' feelings.

38. **Reflect on blunders**: Analyze and learn from past emotional lapses and misjudgments.

39. **Express Gratitude**: Regularly acknowledge and express appreciation for others.

40. **Adaptive Thinking**: Challenge and reframe unfavorable thought habits.

41. **Honest Feedback**: Seek honest feedback from others about your emotional responses.

42. **Adopt a progress Mindset**: Embrace setbacks as chances for personal progress.

43. **Stress Coping Strategies**: Develop healthy plans to cope with stress and adversity.

44. **Active Self-Care**: Prioritize self-care to support your emotional well-being.

45. **Mindful Decision-Making**: Make decisions after evaluating their emotional and long-term repercussions.

46. **Compassionate Self-Talk**: Speak to oneself with care and support.

47. **Family Dynamics**: Understand how family dynamics may have influenced your emotional responses.

48. **Team Building**: Foster emotional intelligence within teams to increase collaboration.

49. **Maintain a Support System**: Surround yourself with supportive, emotionally intelligent persons.

50. **Cultural Awareness**: Educate yourself on cultural variances in emotional expression and communication.

Developing emotional intelligence is an ongoing journey that can lead to enhanced relationships, self-awareness, and general well-being. These recommendations give a tremendous basis for boosting your EI.

Part III

Leading Teams

In this section of our leadership journey, we move our focus to the art of leading teams. Effective leadership isn't only about personal progress; it's about leveraging the collective potential of a group. Throughout this part, we'll discuss tactics and concepts for guiding, motivating, and empowering teams to achieve common goals. From team dynamics and communication to conflict resolution and establishing a positive team culture, we'll delve into the skills and insights you need to be a great team leader. Join us as we examine the mechanics of leading teams toward excellence and collaboration.

Chapter 7

Team Dynamics and Collaboration.

Team dynamics relate to the interpersonal and social interactions that occur within a team. It involves how team members communicate, work together, and influence each other while achieving similar objectives. Team dynamics help hugely in a team's performance and overall achievement.

Collaboration is a crucial part of team dynamics. It involves team members working together cooperatively to achieve shared goals.

Effective teamwork includes:

1. **Open Communication:** Team members openly share information, ideas, and feedback. Clear and honest communication is vital for collaboration.

2. **Position Clarity:** Each team member understands their position and duties. Clarity prevents confusion and overlapping tasks.

3. **Trust and appreciate:** Team members trust each other's abilities and appreciate varied opinions. Trust is the foundation of productive collaboration.

4. **Conflict Resolution:** Teams should have systems in place to manage problems constructively, ensuring that disputes do not inhibit collaboration.

5. **Shared Goals:** Team members are aligned with common objectives and are driven to work toward them collectively.

6. **Friendly Environment:** The team fosters a friendly climate where members feel comfortable expressing ideas and taking risks.

7. **Diversity and Inclusion:** Diverse teams that value varied backgrounds and viewpoints generally succeed in collaboration, since they contribute a larger range of ideas and solutions.

Effective team dynamics and collaboration lead to increased productivity, inventive problem-solving,

and a more favorable team climate. It's about harnessing the capabilities of each team member and building a synergy that increases the team's collective performance.

Chapter 8

Inspiring and Motivating Others

Inspiring and encouraging people can be achieved through the following means stated below:

-Lead by Example: Be a role model by showing the behavior and work ethic you demand from others.

-Effective Communication: Clearly express your vision and expectations. Listen actively to others' thoughts and concerns.

-Encourage Risk-Taking: Create an environment where measured risks are appreciated.

-Set Clear Goals: Define clear, achievable goals that correspond with your vision.

-Encourage Creativity: Allow room for innovation and creative problem-solving.

-Provide Challenges: Assign assignments that foster learning and personal growth.

-Promote Inclusivity: Encourage varied ideas and ensure everyone's voice is heard.

-Provide Autonomy: Allow team members to make decisions within their areas of responsibility.

-Inspire with a Vision: Share a captivating vision that thrills and motivates others.

-Acknowledge Achievements: Recognize and appreciate efforts and achievements openly.

-Promote Healthy Competition: Encourage amicable competition within the team.

-Promote Intrinsic Motivation: Encourage people to find intrinsic motivation for their task.

-Promote Well-Being: Support physical and mental health, emphasizing work-life balance.

-Lead with excitement: Bring energy and excitement to your leadership.

-Keep Learning: Cultivate a culture of constant learning and progress.

Chapter 9

Conflict Resolution

In this chapter, we investigate the skill of settling disagreements within teams and organizations.

Discover effective ideas and techniques to transform disagreements into opportunities for growth and collaboration.

1. **Open Communication:** Encourage honest and open communication to identify the fundamental reasons for problems.
2. **Active Listening:** Listen closely to all people involved, validating their perspectives.

3. **Mediation:** Consider a neutral mediator to facilitate resolution.

4. **Seek Common Ground:** Identify similar goals and values to reconcile divides.

5. **Win-Win Solutions:** Strive for solutions that benefit all stakeholders, fostering teamwork.

6. **Conflict Prevention:** Establish clear expectations and standards to prevent future disagreements.

7. **Empathy:** Develop knowledge of each person's feelings and needs.

8. **Focus on the Issue:** Keep discussions centered on the problem, not personal attacks.

9. **Time-Outs:** Use breaks to temper tensions and gain perspective.

10. **Agree to Disagree:** Sometimes, acceptance of differing ideas is the best resolution.

11. Time Management: Don't rush the resolving procedure. Sometimes, disputes need time to cool off before fruitful discussions may occur.

12. Conflict Analysis: Analyze the root causes of conflicts to solve underlying issues rather than merely surface-level arguments.

13. Celebrate Success: When disagreements are successfully handled and turned into opportunities, acknowledge and celebrate the achievements with all interested parties.

14. Learn from Conflict: View conflict as a chance for learning and growth. Encourage a culture where mistakes and disputes are recognized as opportunities for progress.

15. Training and Education: Provide conflict resolution training for team members to increase their conflict management skills. Teach negotiation skills, such as compromising and creating win-win solutions.

These tactics support conflict resolution that converts discord into an opportunity for personal and social progress.

Part IV

Navigating the Professional Landscape

This is a segment dedicated to preparing individuals with the knowledge and abilities necessary for success in the professional environment.

It includes themes such as professional development, networking, job search tactics, and workplace etiquette, providing vital insights for people commencing or developing in their professions.

Chapter 10

Leading Through Change

Leading Through Change covers the key features of managing and leading teams throughout moments of transition and change within a company. It looks into the necessity of good communication, adaptation, and the capacity to inspire and motivate teams in times of uncertainty. This chapter presents techniques for leaders to navigate change successfully, emphasizing the necessity for a clear vision, a supportive company culture, and the ability to address resistance. It also underlines the importance of leaders in steering their teams towards embracing change as an opportunity for growth and creativity, making it an essential read for those in leadership roles.

Effective communication is of fundamental importance in all parts of life, including personal relationships, education, and especially in professional and corporate environments.

Here are the primary reasons why efficient communication is crucial:

1. **Clarity:** Effective communication ensures that the message is understood correctly, eliminating misunderstandings and misinterpretations.
2. **Conflict Resolution:** It plays a critical role in resolving problems by promoting open communication, understanding, and compromise.
3. **Team cooperation:** In organizations, it enhances cooperation and teamwork, leading to greater problem-solving and innovation.
4. **Decision-Making:** Clear communication offers the required information for informed decision-making, boosting the quality of options.

5. **Productivity:** It boosts productivity by lowering the chances of errors and rework, saving time and resources.

6. **Leadership:** Strong leaders are effective communicators who can inspire, motivate, and align their teams toward common goals.

7. **Customer Relations:** In business, it establishes trust with customers, leading to loyalty and positive brand perception.

8. **Personal Relationships:** Effective communication is the foundation of healthy and happy relationships, generating empathy and connection.

In summary, efficient communication is key to achieving success, whether in personal life, school, or the professional sphere, as it underpins understanding, cooperation, and advancement.

Adaptability is the ability to adjust to changing events and environments. It requires being adaptable, open to new ideas, and resilient in the face of obstacles. To adapt effectively, one should embrace change as a chance for progress, stay attentive to input, and remain proactive. It's vital to acquire problem-solving abilities, a positive mindset, and a willingness to learn. Adapting to conditions typically means assessing the new context, recognizing essential adjustments, and executing them with an open and nimble attitude.

This quality is highly prized in personal and professional life, as it helps individuals to thrive in ever-evolving conditions and seize chances as they emerge.

1. **Clear Vision**: Provide a compelling and clear vision of the team's goals and the route forward.

2. **Open contact**: Foster honest and regular contact to resolve concerns and provide updates.

3. **Empowerment**: Give team members free will and decision-making authority, making them feel valued.

4. **Recognition**: Acknowledge and reward successes, promoting a sense of accomplishment.

5. **Resilience**: Demonstrate resilience in the face of uncertainty, establishing an example for the team.

6. **Learning Culture**: Encourage constant learning and adaptability, promoting progress even in uncertain times.

7. **Support System**: Offer emotional and professional support to team members, showing care for their well-being.

8. **Goal Alignment**: Ensure team goals correspond with individual aspirations and values, improving motivation.

9. **Adaptability**: Embrace change and foster creative problem-solving, turning obstacles into opportunities.

10. **Feedback Loop**: Establish a feedback process for ongoing improvement, empowering the team to make meaningful contributions.

These tactics can jointly inspire and motivate teams to prosper amidst uncertainty.

A supportive organizational culture supports and prioritizes the well-being, progress, and pleasure of its employees. It generates an environment where individuals feel appreciated, included, and empowered to accomplish their best.

Here's how to implement it:

1. **Values and Mission**: Define clear values and a mission statement that stresses a culture of support and respect for employees.

2. **Leadership Role Modeling**: Leaders should set an example by promoting open communication, empathy, and work-life balance.

3. **Communication**: Encourage transparent and open communication within the organization, so employees feel heard and understood.

4. **Employee Development**: Invest in training, career development, and skill upgrading opportunities, encouraging employee growth.

5. **Mentoring and Coaching**: Establish mentoring programs to provide assistance and enhance skill development.

6. **Work-Life Balance**: Promote a healthy work-life balance, avoiding overwork and exhaustion.

7. **Recognition and Rewards**: Implement recognition and reward systems that acknowledge and celebrate employee successes.

8. **Diversity and Inclusion**: Foster diversity and inclusion, fostering a sense of belonging for all employees.

9. **Feedback Channels**: Provide outlets for employees to give feedback and act on their suggestions for improvement.

10. **Empowerment**: Give employees autonomy and decision-making authority, making them feel powerful and trustworthy.

11. **Well-being Initiatives**: Introduce wellness programs and initiatives to enhance physical and mental health.

12. **Conflict Resolution**: Develop effective conflict resolution strategies to address concerns constructively.

13. **Continuous Improvement**: Regularly analyze and alter organizational culture based on input and growing needs. Creating a supportive corporate culture is an ongoing effort that demands commitment from leadership and a real emphasis on the well-being and growth of employees. When effectively applied, it can lead to improved job satisfaction, increased productivity, and a positive reputation in the industry.

Resistance in an organizational setting refers to the reluctance or opposition individuals or groups exhibit when confronted with change. It can emerge as uncertainty, opposition, or even refusal to participate. People resist change because they fear being different--especially when there's no routine,

lack of confidence in the person implementing the change, lack of the skills and training needed to adjust to the change, and many other reasons.

To address resistance effectively, numerous talents are required.

Active listening and empathy are necessary for recognizing concerns, and objections, while excellent communication helps express the reasons and benefits of the change. Involving team members in decision-making and delivering education and training might make them feel more connected to the change.

Conflict resolution and feedback methods are crucial to address concerns constructively. Leadership by example, acknowledging little achievements, and providing coaching and support contribute to a pleasant climate.

Transparency in communication is vital for sustaining confidence, and resilience in the face of resistance.

These abilities collectively assist leaders in managing and lessening resistance, promoting smoother transitions, and getting buy-in for change projects. Leaders play a vital role in persuading their people to perceive change as an opportunity for growth and innovation rather than a threat. First and foremost, they must set an example by displaying their commitment to change and a constructive approach towards it. Leaders should articulate a clear vision for the future, stressing the possible benefits and possibilities that the transition brings. They need to create a secure atmosphere for open communication, encouraging ideas, and addressing issues to build trust. Leaders may inspire innovation by establishing a culture that values experimentation and learning from failure. They should encourage team members to take ownership of the change process, providing the liberty and resources needed to explore new ideas and approaches. Recognizing and appreciating both individual and collective achievements in adjusting to change can increase morale and motivation. In doing so, leaders not only help their staff navigate uncertainty but also create an attitude of continual growth and innovation, assuring the organization's long-term success.

Chapter 11

Decision-Making and Problem-Solving

Decision-making and issue-solving are vital components of personal and professional life.

They involve numerous key elements:

1. **Identifying the Problem**: The first step is acknowledging the issue or difficulty at hand. A precise problem definition is necessary for efficient problem-solving.

2. **Information Gathering**: Collecting relevant data and information is crucial to comprehending the situation fully.

3. **Generating Alternatives**: Brainstorming alternative solutions or courses of action creates a range of options.

4. **Evaluating Options**: Consider the pros and cons of each possibility, taking into account repercussions, risks, and advantages.

5. **Conclusion Making**: Choose the best answer based on the evaluation, making a well-informed conclusion.

6. **Implementation**: Put the choice into action, establishing a plan and committing resources.

7. **Monitoring and Adjustment**: Continuously review the results and be ready to alter the plan as needed.

8. **Critical Thinking**: Apply logical and critical thinking abilities to assess situations and make judgments.

9. **Time Management**: Efficiently allocate time for each step of the decision-making process.

10. **Collaboration**: Seek input from others, as collaborative decision-making typically leads to more well-rounded answers.

11. **Risk Management**: Assess and mitigate potential risks connected with the chosen decision.

12. **Ethical Considerations**: Ensure decisions correspond with ethical and moral principles.

13. **Creativity**: Embrace creativity in issue-solving to consider unconventional solutions.

14. **Data-Driven Decisions**: Use data and evidence to inform decisions whenever possible.

15. **Communication**: Effectively communicate decisions to important stakeholders.

Both decision-making and problem-solving are iterative processes that need adaptability and learning from experiences. Effective mastery of these talents is vital for personal and professional success.

Chapter 12

Networking and Building Relationships

Networking and building relationships are crucial in both personal and professional life. Networking means interacting with individuals to exchange information, support, and opportunities. Building relationships is the foundation of successful networking.

Here are crucial elements to consider:

1. **Professional Networking**: In the corporate world, networking can open doors to professional prospects, partnerships, and collaborations.

2. **Personal Networking**: Building contacts outside of work is crucial for personal growth, social support, and a satisfying existence.

3. **Authenticity**: Be genuine and authentic in your interactions. Authenticity fosters trust and better bonds.

4. **Listening Skills**: Be an engaged listener. Pay attention to people and show genuine interest in their views and wants.

5. **Reciprocity**: Networking is a two-way street. Offer help and support to others in addition to seeking it for yourself.

6. **Online Networking**: Utilize social media platforms and online communities to connect with people in your field of interest.

7. **Events and Conferences**: Attend industry events, conferences, and meetings to meet new people and develop current contacts.

8. **Follow-Up**: After initial contact, follow up with your network to foster relationships and keep them engaged.

9 **Mentorship**: Seek mentors and offer mentorship to others. Mentors can provide direction and insights.

10. **Diversity**: Build a diversified network to acquire new viewpoints and chances.

11.. **Value Proposition**: Understand what you can give to your network. Your talents, expertise, and experiences can be beneficial to others.

12. **Maintaining limits**: Maintain professional and personal limits in your dealings.

13. **Long-Term Perspective**: Networking is a continuing activity, not merely a means to an instant end. Invest in long-term partnerships.

14. **Gratitude**: Show appreciation to your network. A simple thank you can go a long way in developing solid ties.

15. Purpose and Goals: Define your objectives for networking. Are you seeking job possibilities, mentorship, or personal growth?

16. Leverage Existing Contacts: Start by reaching out to your present network, including friends, family, and colleagues.

Networking and building relationships involve effort and patience, but the benefits are enormous. It can lead to new opportunities, personal improvement, and a supportive community. Building a healthy network is an invaluable tool in today's interconnected world.

Part V

Achieving Professional Success

Achieving Professional Success is an illuminating journey into the tactics, insights, and attitudes required to flourish in the world of work. This area is a rich trove of information, offering counsel on job progression, leadership, personal development, and the art of realizing one's maximum potential.

Whether you're a seasoned professional or just starting your career, these pages are a roadmap to navigating the complexity of the professional scene and attaining your objectives. Get ready to uncover the keys to success and go on a journey that leads to your professional dreams.

Chapter 13

Goal Setting and Time Management

Goal Setting and **Time Management** are key abilities that help individuals reach their objectives efficiently.

Goal Setting: This is the preparation of an action plan devised to encourage and steer a person or group toward a goal. Goals are deliberate intentions. Therefore, setting objectives signifies that a person has dedicated thought, emotion, and conduct toward obtaining the goal.

Here are the important steps, recommendations, and methods for each:

1. **SMART Goals**: Make your goals Specific, Measurable, Achievable, Relevant, and Time-bound.
2. **Long-Term and Short-Term Goals**: Set both long-term aims and short-term objectives to keep your focus balanced.

3. **Prioritization**: Rank your goals in order of importance to allocate time and effort wisely.
4. **Write Them Down**: Putting your goals on paper enhances dedication and clarity.
5. **Break Them Down**: Divide larger goals into smaller, doable steps or milestones.

6. **Visualize Success**: Imagine attaining your goals; this helps improve motivation.

7. **Regular Review**: Periodically evaluate and revise your goals as circumstances change.

8. **Accountability**: Share your goals with a trustworthy friend or mentor who can hold you accountable.

Time Management: Time management is the process of organizing and planning how to split your time between different activities. Get it correctly, and you'll wind up working smarter, not harder, to get more done in less time.

Below are some strategies and tips to manage your time successfully and efficiently:

1. **Prioritization**: Identify high-priority tasks and address them first.

2. **To-Do Lists**: Create daily or weekly to-do lists to keep organized.

3. **Time Blocking**: Allocate specified time blocks for tasks, minimizing distractions.

4. **Set Deadlines**: Establish deadlines for each work to keep concentration and prevent procrastination.

5. **Batching**: Group related tasks together to enhance efficiency.

6. **Avoid Multitasking**: Focus on one task at a time for better results.

7. **Eliminate Time-Wasters**: Identify and minimize activities that take time without contributing value.

8. **Delegate**: Assign chores to others when possible to free up your time for higher-priority work.

9. **Learn to Say No**: Don't overcommit; be selective about taking on new duties.

10. **Self-Care**: Ensure time for rest, relaxation, and personal well-being to maintain productivity.

11. **Technology Tools**: Utilize time management applications and tools for planning and tracking work.

12. **Continuous Improvement**: Reflect on your time management tactics often and make improvements as needed.

Balancing goal setting and time management is vital for reaching your ambitions efficiently. Setting well-defined goals provides a sense of purpose, while efficient time management ensures that you make continuous progress toward those goals.

Chapter 14

Continuous Learning and Growth

Continuous Learning and Growth is a lifelong journey to personal and professional improvement. It explores the transforming potential of lifelong learning, offering insights, solutions, and inspiration for individuals devoted to evolving, adapting, and thriving in an ever-changing environment. This chapter provides a guide to embracing curiosity, developing new abilities, and fostering a mindset of progress, ensuring that your road of self-improvement never ends.

Indeed, obtaining new skills, knowledge, and experiences is the cornerstone of personal and professional progress. In an ever-evolving world, the ability to adapt and learn continuously is vital. It gives individuals the tools to succeed in dynamic

circumstances, stay relevant in their careers, and realize their full potential.

New skills strengthen your capacities, while information broadens your viewpoints. Experiences bring essential lessons and insights.
Together, they help you to overcome uncertainty, grasp opportunities, and consistently improve both personally and professionally. Ongoing learning

develops innovation, creativity, and resilience, ultimately leading to a more successful and meaningful life. Embracing this principle is a method to not only keep pace with change but also stay ahead of it.

Chapter 15

Leading with Integrity

Firstly, what is integrity? This is the attribute of being honest and having strong moral beliefs.

Leading with integrity is crucial for both personal and professional success.

Importance of Leading with Integrity:

1. **Trust and Credibility**: Integrity is the foundation of trust. Leaders with integrity win the trust and respect of their team, colleagues, and stakeholders, which is crucial for effective leadership.

2. **Ethical Compass**: It creates a clear ethical compass for decision-making, ensuring that decisions align with moral and ethical values.

3. **Long-Term Success**: Leaders with integrity establish lasting relationships and organizations, fostering long-term success.

4. **Positive Culture**: They build a culture of honesty and accountability, encouraging ethical behavior throughout the team.

5. **Dispute settlement**: Integrity assists in fair and constructive dispute settlement, providing a healthy work atmosphere.

Steps to Leading with Integrity:

1. **Self-Reflection**: Understand your values and ideals. Reflect on what integrity means to you.

2. **Lead by Example**: Demonstrate integrity in your acts, words, and decisions. Be a role model for ethical behavior.
Display attitudes that you want your team to emulate and also establish rules of conduct for every staff to observe, stating what actions won't be tolerated

3. **Transparency**: Maintain transparent communication, sharing information openly and honestly.

4. **Accountability**: Hold yourself accountable for your actions and decisions, and demand the same from your team.

5. **Consistency**: Be consistent in your behavior and decision-making. Avoid favoritism or bias.

6. **Ethical Decision-Making**: When facing ethical problems, prioritize doing what is right over what is simple or convenient.

7. **Listen Actively**: Listen to others' concerns and feedback, and answer with empathy and respect.

8. **Empower Whistleblowers**: Encourage reporting of unethical behavior and protect whistleblowers from reprisal.

9. **Continuous Improvement**: Regularly examine your leadership for areas where you may better integrate integrity into your approach.

10. **Seek input**: Request input from peers, mentors, and coworkers to help you grow as an ethical leader.

11. **Moral Courage**: Be willing to stand up for your values, especially in the face of adversity or opposition.

Leading with integrity not only ensures ethical conduct but also inspires those you lead to act with integrity. It promotes a culture of trust, respect, and accountability, eventually contributing to the long-term success and well-being of your team and business.

Conclusion

In **"Supercharge Your Leadership"** we find ourselves at the summit of an inspiring voyage. The book's narrative, interwoven with wisdom and practical guidance, has taken readers on a transformative exploration of what it truly means to lead.As we reach the final chapter, it emerges as a beacon of empowerment and inspiration. It becomes abundantly obvious that authentic leadership is not merely about titles or authority; it's a profound understanding of self, a commitment to continuous growth, and a genuine desire to uplift others.

It echoes as a compelling call to action, encouraging readers to put into practice all the principles and insights.

The true satisfaction resides not in reaching an endpoint but in embracing the knowledge that the path to individual power and professional success is an ongoing, changing journey. It's a journey marked by resilience, adaptability, and the ability to ignite positive change.In the end, readers are left with a

sense of fulfillment and empowerment. Armed with newfound wisdom, they are ready to step confidently into their leadership roles, guided by their unique strengths, nurturing meaningful connections, and leaving a lasting legacy of authenticity and compassion.

"Supercharge Your Leadership" serves as a catalyst for readers to commence on their leadership journeys, poised to make a profound and enduring impact in their personal and professional lives.

Appendix

Additional Resources for Leadership Mastery

Congratulations on embarking on your voyage toward Leadership Mastery!

This appendix functions as a valuable resource guide, offering further tools, references, and recommendations to support your ongoing development as a leader.

1. Recommended Books:

- "Leaders Eat Last" by Simon Sinek: Explore the concept of selfless leadership and how it can transform organizations.

- "Dare to Lead" by Brené Brown: Delve into the power of vulnerability and courage in leadership.

- "The 7 Habits of Highly Effective People" by Stephen R. Covey: Learn timeless principles for personal and professional effectiveness.

"Primal Leadership" by Daniel Goleman.

- "Leadership and the New Science: Discovering Order in a Chaotic World" by Margaret Wheatley.

  - "101 Reasons to Get Out of Bed" by Natasha Milne

2. Online Courses and Training:

- Coursera (www.coursera.org): Access a variety of leadership courses from top universities and institutions.

- LinkedIn Learning (www.linkedin.com/learning): Explore a vast library of leadership-related courses.

- EdX (www.edx.org): Enroll in leadership and management courses from universities and institutions worldwide.

3. Leadership Podcasts:

"The Tony Robbins Podcast": Gain insights from Tony Robbins on leadership, personal growth, and business.

- "The Leadership Podcast" by The Leadership Podcast: Explore diverse perspectives on leadership and management.

4. Leadership Assessment Tools:

- Myers-Briggs Type Indicator (MBTI): Understand your personality type and how it relates to your leadership approach.

- StrengthsFinder: Identify your distinctive strengths and how to leverage them for leadership success.

-The Center for Creative Leadership (CCL): CCL is an organization that provides various leadership

assessment tools and resources. Their website and publications are valuable sources of information.

5. Mentorship and Coaching: Consider seeking a mentor or leadership coach who can provide personalized guidance and support on your journey.

6. Professional Associations: Join industry-specific or general leadership organizations to connect with like-minded professionals and remain updated on leadership trends and best practices.

7. Leadership Conferences: Attend leadership conferences and seminars to network and learn from industry leaders.

8. Online Communities: Engage in online forums and communities dedicated to leadership and management discussions.

9. Continuing Education: Consider pursuing advanced degrees or certifications in leadership and

management to deepen your knowledge and credentials.

10. Networking: Actively build and maintain a professional network to exchange ideas, experiences, and opportunities with other executives.

Remember that leadership is an ongoing voyage, and the pursuit of mastery is a lifelong endeavor. Use these resources to continue expanding your knowledge, refining your abilities, and making a lasting impact as a leader. May your path to Leadership Mastery be both fulfilling and inspiring.

Note: Please verify the availability and suitability of these resources to your specific needs and goals.

www.ingramcontent.com/pod-product-compliance
Lightning Source LLC
Chambersburg PA
CBHW072340290526
45794CB00002B/960